CW01512508

Original title:
Dull Capers Beneath the Dragon Barb

Author: Paulina Pähkel
ISBN HARDBACK: 978-1-80562-908-5
ISBN PAPERBACK: 978-1-80564-429-3

The Final Performance in Starlit Ash

In halls where echoes softly play,
The shadows dance, the night holds sway.
A stage adorned with twilight's grace,
Each whisper woven, a timeless trace.

Upon the boards where dreams take flight,
Illumined by the silver light.
An audience of stars do gaze,
As magic stirs in twilight's haze.

With vengeful hearts and tender tears,
The stories spun through fleeting years.
A tale reborn of love and loss,
In ashes bright, the dreams embossed.

The actors sway like willow trees,
Caught in the spell of ancient breeze.
Each word a spell, a brush on skin,
They conjure worlds both dark and thin.

As final notes begin to fade,
The stardust trails in whispers laid.
And in this night where shadows clash,
We part with grace, our starlit ash.

Whispers of the Gloomy Tides

In the murmur of the waves, so low,
Secrets of the deep begin to flow,
A siren's song, both sweet and dire,
Calls forth the dreams, igniting fire.

The moon hangs heavy, draped in dread,
Its silver shimmer on waters spread,
Beneath the surface, shadows creep,
And stories long forgotten, keep.

A fog ensnares the distant shore,
While whispers linger evermore,
Each tide that rises, curls in fright,
Brings forth the echoes of lost light.

Yet in the gloom, a flicker glows,
A spark of hope the heart bestows,
With every wave, the past will fade,
And in its place, new tales are made.

So heed the call of tempest's roar,
The whispers tell of ancient lore,
For in the depths where darkness bides,
Are treasures lost within the tides.

Shadows Dance in the Ashen Light

In the twilight's soft embrace, they sway,
Figures lost, where dreams decay,
The shadows fan the ember's glow,
Whispers of secrets nobody knows.

Beneath the sky, a canvas torn,
Where hope lies broken, dreams forlorn,
In every flicker, a dance so grim,
With echoes that haunt the edges dim.

The ash falls gently, like a sigh,
Carrying whispers of the sky,
Each movement slow, yet filled with grace,
A haunting waltz in time and space.

Yet within chaos, a heartbeat cries,
Reminding all that love never dies,
For every shadow shall find its light,
And dance again, with renewed might.

So listen close to the beauty found,
In the ashen light where dreams abound,
For even shadows have tales to weave,
In every heart that dares to believe.

Lament of the Somber Revelers

In the halls where laughter used to ring,
Now echoes fade, and shadows cling,
The revelers clad in sorrow's veil,
Invisible chains drag their frail tale.

They raise their cups to the fleeting night,
But each sip numbs, it dims the light,
With every cheer, a silent plea,
For joy long lost, for hearts set free.

Distant music haunts the air,
A bittersweet tune of despair,
As merriment cloaks each hidden tear,
In every smile, a glimpse of fear.

Yet among the throng, a flicker glows,
A spark of hope where sadness flows,
A reminder that amidst the gloom,
The dance of life will find its bloom.

So toast the night with heavy hearts,
For even sorrowed souls play parts,
In the lament of the somber crowd,
Joy and grief entwined, unbowed.

Gritted Teeth and Stifled Laughs

Beneath the mask of smiles and glee,
Lie gritted teeth, a silent plea,
For laughter's edge, so sharp and bright,
Can camouflage the deepest fright.

In crowded rooms, the faces blend,
But in each heart, the shadows mend,
With every chuckle, a weight is tossed,
Yet inside, the warmth feels lost.

The banter flows like wine so sweet,
Yet in the depths, the sorrows meet,
A jest, a jibe, a carefree fling,
Hides burdens that the silence brings.

So every laugh has its own tale,
In hidden depths, where spirits pale,
As joy and pain embrace the dark,
And find their way, igniting sparks.

But in this dance of grief and cheer,
A truth emerges, strong and clear,
In every jest, a battle fought,
In laughter's depths, resilience sought.

Mischief in the Grip of Silence

Whispers dance in empty halls,
Where shadows stretch and secrets call.
A flicker gleams in the eerie night,
With every heartbeat, a spell takes flight.

In corners dark, mischief brews,
Trickster spirits sing their blues.
Where laughter hides behind a mask,
In silence, secrets dare to bask.

Autumn leaves swirl in a playful breeze,
As moonlight plays with twisted trees.
Echoes of giggles, faint and clear,
Lift the veil of creeping fear.

A riddle waits in the quiet dusk,
Wrapped in laughter, sweet, and brisk.
With every pause, the silence grows,
In its grip, the mischief flows.

Unraveled Threads of Gloomy Delight

In twilight's grasp, the threads unwind,
Of tales untold, both cruel and kind.
Emotions weave a tapestry bright,
While shadows beckon with their might.

A thread of sorrow binds us tight,
Yet hope remains, a flickering light.
Through faded whispers, hearts entwine,
In gloomy delight, we find the divine.

Masked in gloom, the laughter blooms,
Like wildflowers in forgotten rooms.
A melody soft, a haunting refrain,
In the stillness, we dance through the pain.

Each twist and turn, a story spun,
From glimmers of dusk to rise of sun.
In tangled knots of fate, we sway,
Embracing joy in the shadows' play.

Fragments of Laughter in the Mist

Through veils of fog, the giggles cling,
Like whispers lost on the breath of spring.
In every corner, delight takes flight,
A waltz of joy in the pale twilight.

Echoes flutter, a soft refrain,
Where joy and sorrow intertwine in vain.
The dance of shadows, the shimmering light,
A mosaic of laughter in the night.

Each glimmering tear, a story shared,
In the tapestry woven, both loved and scared.
Through every fragment that fades from sight,
A memory glows, forever bright.

Misty veils conceal the play,
Yet laughter teases the gloom away.
In fleeting moments, we find our bliss,
In the fragments of laughter, we dare to kiss.

Galas with a Veil of Ash

In opulent halls where shadows lie,
Galas unfold under starlit sky.
With grandeur clad in layers of ash,
The laughter sparkles, a shimmering flash.

Beneath the masks, a story's told,
Of dreams once bright, now faint and cold.
In elegance dressed, the guests await,
As whispers drift through the hands of fate.

The music plays, a haunting tune,
Where hearts collide beneath the moon.
In every glance, the hidden desires,
Fueling hope amidst funeral pyres.

Through swirling smoke, the night reveals,
Fragments of life with their spinning wheels.
A gala of ashes, yet souls set free,
In the dance of shadows, we find our glee.

Traces of Fun in the Dragon's Keep

In the heart of stone and scales,
Laughter dances like the wind,
Echoes of tales where magic prevails,
And dreams of daring quests begin.

Sparkling glimmers in the night,
Wondrous games of wits and charms,
Each corner whispers pure delight,
Where dragonkind spread their arms.

With playful roars that shake the skies,
In layers of history they unfold,
From ancient breath, a youthful rise,
As secrets of the keep are told.

Golden glints on treasure's edge,
Where friendships bloom in cozy nooks,
Adventures spring from every pledge,
In dragon's lair, the world unlocks.

Ephemeral Jests Amongst Fading Flames

In twilight's embrace, the fire glows,
Whispers of laughter swirl around,
As embers dance in delicate shows,
And heartbeats echo with joy profound.

Each flicker tells a story bright,
Of fleeting smiles and mischief grand,
A tapestry spun in the night,
By hands unseen, yet truly planned.

Moments captured in blush of flame,
Like petals scattered on the breeze,
Every jest a friend's sweet claim,
In the warmth, we find our ease.

So let the night weave its magic thrice,
While starlight wraps its gentle glow,
For in this dance, we pay the price,
And treasure moments before they go.

The Resilient Gleam of Starlit Embers

Through ages past, the story shines,
Each ember sparked from ancient light,
Resilience held in tangled vines,
A heart that beats against the night.

With every glow, a tale rewrites,
Of dreams ignited, hopes restored,
In starlit realms where magic bites,
The echoes of our hearts, adored.

For every shadow that descends,
A spirit battles, fierce and true,
Together, laughter never ends,
In every spark, a world anew.

Embers gleam like wishes cast,
Upon the canvas of the sky,
Through trials known, we hold steadfast,
With starlit dreams that never die.

In the Wake of Dragonfire Shadows

From the blaze that lights the morn,
Shadows stretch in fiery grace,
Every tale of magic born,
With dragon's breath, an ancient trace.

In the wake of flames that roar,
Whispers flutter in the breeze,
Legends carved on ash-strewn floor,
As night falls softly, hearts find ease.

With every ember softly sparking,
Secrets flow through twilight's seams,
In the night, adventure harking,
A world awakened from its dreams.

So let us roam through shifting light,
In shadows mixed with golden fire,
For in the dark, emerges bright,
The dance of myths that never tire.

Tread Softly in the Dragon's Domain

In the heart of the forest, where shadows creep,
Lies a world of whispers, secrets to keep.
With scales that glisten, fierce eyes aglow,
A dragon lies waiting, its breath like a blow.

For each step you take, tread gently, be wise,
For the whispering leaves tell tales of the skies.
The air is thick with magic, a palpable thrill,
As the ground beneath echoes a soft, ancient chill.

With fire in its heart, it watches you near,
The pulse of the night brings both hope and fear.
A flick of its tail sends tremors through land,
In this realm of legends, few dare to stand.

So gather your courage, oh wayward dreamer,
For danger and wonder weave every steamer.
And when the night falls, let your spirit take flight,
For each flame tells a story of bravery and light.

Songs of Ash and Moonlit Grief

In the stillness of night, where shadows entwine,
The ashes of memories whisper in rhyme.
With a voice like a sigh, the dark softly weeps,
Echoes of sorrows a restless heart keeps.

Beneath the cold gaze of the silver-lit moon,
Grief dances like flames, to an old, haunting tune.
Each flicker remembers the love that was lost,
The warmth that once thrived, now an ice-bound frost.

Yet among the soft whispers, a silver thread glows,
Binding the past with the strength of the prose.
For longing is not just a shackle or chain,
But a bridge to the soul, through joy and through pain.

As shadows unfold, and time holds its breath,
The heart finds its rhythm, even in death.
For love is eternal, its echo shall last,
In the songs of the night, where the veils are cast.

In the Grip of Twilight's Reprieve

When twilight descends, and the world holds its sigh,
The skies blend in colors, a soft lullaby.
The stars weave their stories, like threads in the sky,
While shadows awaken, and dreams start to fly.

In the hush of the dusk, where the echoes collide,
Lies a moment of stillness where secrets can bide.
For beneath the dim light, new tales start to weave,
In the grip of the twilight, we dare to believe.

As night wraps its arms around all that we know,
The magic stirs gently, begins to grow.
With a flick of the wand, and a heart open wide,
Each whisper of dusk is a chance to confide.

So linger in twilight, where wishes take flight,
For the grip of its charm will carry you bright.
In the silence, a promise, a door to explore,
Where the heart finds its rhythm, forever, evermore.

Shadows Danced on Ancient Wings

In the twilight's embrace, where the old stories breathe,
The shadows take form, as the ancients bequeath.
With wings made of whispers, they flutter and glide,
Through realms of the forgotten, where dreams dare to hide.

A flicker of starlight ignites the night sky,
Drawing forth memories that flutter on high.
They swirl in the silence, both gentle and bold,
Every tale they carry is a wonder retold.

In the realm of the echoes, where magic is spun,
The dance of the shadows is never quite done.
With each breath of the night, new journeys take flight,
As the stories weave together, they birth new insight.

So listen, dear dreamer, to the soft whispers call,
For shadows of old have a wisdom for all.
In the flutter of wings, find the paths yet unseen,
As the night sings of wonders that dance in between.

Foretelling Tales from the Great Divide

Beneath the bridge where fate entwines,
The whispers of the past define.
Dreamers cast their shadows long,
As time reveals its haunting song.

In twilight's glow, the secrets creep,
Each tale spun, the echoes deep.
With every step, the stories breathe,
Lurking where the brave believe.

Among the stars, the lost unite,
A flicker in the endless night.
With mirrored hearts, the worlds collide,
Unraveling the Great Divide.

A tapestry of dreams once sewn,
In threads of starlight overgrown.
The echoes rustle through the trees,
Inviting all to hear and seize.

From ancient lore, the songs arise,
And rise they do, like fireflies.
Foretelling fates both grim and grand,
In whispers lost, or futures planned.

The Mirth of Shadows and Cinders

Among the glowing embers bright,
The shadows dance with pure delight.
A laughter weaves through night's embrace,
As fireflies flit in joyful chase.

With every spark, a story born,
Of whispered hopes and dreams forlorn.
The flickers play, their secrets keep,
Awake to humor woven deep.

In cinders' glow, the past ignites,
Embodying both sparks and frights.
They twirl and twist in cheeky glee,
As shadows share their mystery.

Beneath the sky where wild winds blow,
The echoing laughter starts to flow.
With every grin, the darkness lifts,
And in the gloom, a gift exists.

So heed the mirth that shadows bring,
For even darkness can take wing.
In laughter's warmth, we find our way,
Through night's embrace, and into day.

Wondrous Frolics Under the Gloom

A waltz of whispers fills the air,
As creatures tread without a care.
With twinkling eyes and hearts aflame,
They dance beneath a moonlit frame.

In shadows thick, the secrets hide,
And in their midst, the dreams collide.
Each flutter brings a tale anew,
In every shade, a vibrant hue.

Through gnarled trees, the laughter flows,
Where night-time stillness gently glows.
With every step, the world awakes,
In wondrous frolics, joy remakes.

The echoes of the mystic night,
Like stars that twinkle, bold and bright.
They call to all who dare to roam,
To find their heart, to seek their home.

So join the dance, embrace the night,
In every shadow, find the light.
Through gloom and mist, let spirits rise,
And in the dark, claim your reprise.

Emotions Entwined in Charred Remnants

Among the ashes, memories dwell,
Of love once sparked and stories tell.
In every ember, a sigh remains,
Of passions lost, of bittersweet gains.

With charcoal hearts, we brave the flames,
In every tear, a story claims.
Entwined in pain, yet hope ignites,
A dance through shadows, seeking lights.

While charred remnants whisper low,
The echoes of what we used to know.
In tragic grace, we find our way,
Through trials faced, and choices made.

Yet in the ruins, life renews,
A chance to rise, to seek the blues.
With every heartbeat, we reclaim,
The strength to rise, to love the same.

So cherish all that fire has burned,
For in its wake, new lessons learned.
In charred remains, our spirits soar,
Emotions twined, forevermore.

The Unseen Path Through Fire and Stone

In shadows deep where whispers tread,
Beneath the weight of dreams long shed.
The echoes call from distant lands,
Where courage stirs in silent sands.

A flicker bright, like embers glow,
A secret trail where few dare go.
Through flames that dance and stones that lie,
The heart must soar, the spirit fly.

With every step, the old ones sigh,
Their tales entwined in stardust sky.
Through trials fierce, the brave shall find,
The path unseen, by fate aligned.

As night descends, the stars ignite,
Guiding souls through darkened flight.
To realms where hope and fear conjoin,
The fire's warmth becomes the coin.

At journey's end, the truth revealed,
In every wound, the strength concealed.
Through fire and stone, the wanderers roam,
Unseen paths lead our hearts back home.

Distant Drums of the Hidden Marsh

In twilight's cloak, the drums resound,
An ancient beat from hallowed ground.
Where whispers linger, shadows creep,
The secrets of the marsh enfold and keep.

The reeds stand tall in emerald pride,
Guardians of the dreams inside.
With every thud, the echoes swell,
A haunting rhythm, a timeless spell.

Beneath the moon, the waters sigh,
Reflecting tales of days gone by.
Each splash and ripple, a dance of fate,
Invisible hands at destiny's gate.

In the stillness, a voice will rise,
A call to those who seek the skies.
To listen close and follow near,
The distant drums, a path to steer.

As misty shadows weave and twine,
The hidden marsh reveals its sign.
In twilight's dance, the heart beats true,
To heed the call, to start anew.

Echoes of Feasts in the Wilderness

In wild woods where laughter roams,
Beneath the boughs, where joy finds homes.
The echoes of a feast once shared,
Dance on the breeze, a bond declared.

With every bite, the stories bloom,
The hearths aglow within the gloom.
A bounty spread on nature's plate,
The heart recalls what dreams create.

Under starlit skies, the voices cheer,
Old tales and songs for all to hear.
With every sip, the ties entwine,
As memories flow, a vintage fine.

Laughter mingles with the night,
In wilderness, a pure delight.
The feasts may fade, the fire cool,
But echoes remain, a golden rule.

In nature's arms, our spirits lift,
The bond of kinship, a precious gift.
Through echoes of feasts, our souls combine,
In every heart, a love divine.

Glimmers of Joy in the Gritty Depths

In depths where shadows clasp the ground,
Amid the grit, faint joys are found.
A flicker here, a spark of light,
Awakens dreams in endless night.

With weary hands and battered seams,
We sew together our whispered dreams.
Through trials faced and burdens borne,
The heart finds beauty; all is reborn.

Each stumble, a lesson etched in stone,
In gritty depths, we're never alone.
For every sorrow, a laughter springs,
With every wound, a new hope sings.

In darkness thick, the glimmers play,
A guiding star when skies are gray.
Through winding paths, the light does dance,
In the gritty depths, we take our chance.

As dawn breaks soft, the world awakens,
From hidden sorrows, light is taken.
In glimmers found, we rise anew,
Embracing joy, our hearts break through.

Beneath the Cloak of the Fabled Beast

In shadows deep, a whisper soared,
A tale of old, where magic roared.
A cloak of night, a beast untamed,
In legends lost, their fury claimed.

With eyes aglow, the forest sighed,
In ancient woods, where secrets hide.
Beneath the cloak, a truth is sewn,
In every heart, the dream is known.

A glimmer bright amidst the gloom,
An echoing pulse, a heart to bloom.
The fabled one awaits its time,
To rise again, its strength to climb.

Upon the hill, where shadows play,
The beast will rise to greet the day.
With gentle grace, it breaks the spell,
And weaves the tale we wish to tell.

A bond of fate, a spirit's dance,
In twilight's breath, we take our chance.
Together we shall brave the night,
Beneath the cloak, we find the light.

Meadows of Ash in the Dragon's Breath

Across the plains, where embers gleam,
The fields lie bare, a haunting dream.
In dragon's breath, the ashes fall,
A whisper soft, a distant call.

The meadows once held blooms so bright,
Now shrouded deep in dusky light.
A fire's song, a tale of woe,
Where once was life, now shadows grow.

The echoes linger in the air,
A promise lost, a fading prayer.
Yet from the ash, a spark will rise,
In molten glow, the hope replies.

With every gust, the stories weave,
Of hearths that glow and hearts that grieve.
From dragon's breath, new worlds will bloom,
In fertile ground, dispelling gloom.

So let us stroll through fields of grey,
And speak the words that heal the day.
For in the ashes, seeds are sown,
In meadows rich, we'll find our home.

Whispers Caught in the Ashen Breeze

In silent woods, the secrets flow,
Like streams of thought that softly grow.
Caught in the breeze, a phantom sound,
Of places lost, where dreams abound.

The ashen mist, it wraps around,
Each moment past, a bond unbound.
With lighter hearts, we chase the dusk,
In whispered tales, our souls entrust.

Secrets sleep beneath the earth,
In shadows wide, they find their worth.
To listen close, one must believe,
In every sigh, the air may cleave.

With every breeze, the echoes sing,
Of bygone days and forgotten spring.
Through ash and smoke, we'll carve a path,
In whispered tones, we'll find our math.

Let not the silence bind us tight,
For in the dark, we seek the light.
In every breeze, we'll find our way,
Through whispers caught, we'll seize the day.

Lanterns of Hope Amidst Sooty Veils

When night descends with sooty veils,
And every star seems lost in trails.
The lanterns glow, a gentle guide,
In darkened worlds, where hopes reside.

With flickering flames, our fears are tamed,
Each heart alight, no longer shamed.
We gather round, with laughter bright,
In shadows deep, we find our light.

Amongst the gloom, the lanterns sway,
A dance of dreams that lights the way.
With every flicker, stories bloom,
In every heart, dispelling gloom.

So let us walk 'neath skies so dim,
With lanterns held, our spirits brim.
Through sooty veils, we'll weave our fate,
In hope's embrace, we'll celebrate.

When dawn breaks through, the shadows flee,
And in the light, we're finally free.
With lanterns bright, we've carved our space,
In every heart, a warm embrace.

Fleeting Shadows Through Embered Haze

In the forest where shadows creep,
Whispers gather, secrets keep.
Glimmers dance on emerald leaves,
As twilight beckons, the heart believes.

Fleeting forms in the amber glow,
Shapes of wonders, soft and slow.
Laughter echoes, a wistful sigh,
The night holds dreams as it slips by.

Beneath the stars, fireflies twirl,
Their gentle light begins to unfurl.
Magic stirs in the cooling air,
Embracing all with tender care.

Through the haze of the dying day,
Fleeting moments slip away.
Yet in the dusk, a spark ignites,
A bond eternal amid the night.

So let us wander, hand in hand,
Through breathing woods, a mystic land.
For in these shadows, we'll always find,
An everlasting love, entwined.

Whispers of Twilight in the Scaled Kin

In the dusk where legends rise,
Scaled kin dance beneath the skies.
With eyes like coals, they gleam and glow,
Whispers of twilight, mysteries flow.

Through the mist where dragons soar,
Ancient tales and secrets pour.
Fanning flames with a flick of tail,
Each heartbeat echoes, a timeless tale.

Crimson scales in the fading light,
Guardians born of the stars' own flight.
With every roar, their stories told,
Of ages past, of blazing gold.

In hidden caves, the echoes ring,
A symphony of the wild they bring.
With every flicker, a spirit's cheer,
In this twilight hour, they draw us near.

So gather close, heed the call,
For scaled kin roam in the shadowed hall.
In the whispers of night, together we tread,
To the echoes of dreams our hearts are led.

Echoes of Timber and Dragonflight

In a realm where the tall trees sway,
Echoes linger from far away.
Timber speaks of ancient ties,
Where spirits linger, old and wise.

With wings that stretch across the sky,
Dragons weave as they soar high.
Their roars resound through valley bends,
In this place where magic transcends.

Each rustle of leaf, each hollow sigh,
Holds the stories of those who fly.
With every beat of a mighty wing,
The forest hums, the world takes wing.

Through shadows cast by the setting sun,
Timber stands, its work is done.
While dragons spiral, wild and free,
Together bound by destiny.

So listen close, for the night is rife,
With echoes of timber and dragonflight.
In every breeze, in every tone,
Is the heartbeat of a world grown.

Forgotten Revels in the Firelight

In the circle where shadows dance,
Forgotten revels, a fleeting glance.
Flames flicker, casting tales anew,
Of laughter shared and dreams pursued.

Chanted songs of a world unseen,
Woven tales in a glimmering sheen.
Time stands still as the embers glow,
In the warmth of friendship's gentle flow.

Each fire crackles with memories old,
As stories spin, and hearts unfold.
The night ignites with a vibrant beat,
In this haven where souls meet.

With every crackle, a secret shared,
Connections forged, none unprepared.
Through the firelight, shadows leap,
Guarding memories we hold steep.

So let us gather 'round the flame,
And in our hearts, we'll know the name.
For in forgotten revels, love takes flight,
A tapestry woven in the firelight.

Murmurs of the Smoke-laden Air

In the haze where whispers play,
The night entwines with the day.
Faint echoes dance with the dew,
Secrets of old drifting through.

Shadows stretch across the ground,
In silence, lost souls are found.
Threads of twilight softly sing,
Of dreams that night may yet bring.

Ghostly figures twirl and sway,
In a world where phantoms lay.
With each breath, a tale unfolds,
In the air where fate beholds.

Murmurs flicker, a ghostly tide,
With every sigh, they confide.
In smoke-laden air, we wander,
Bound by whispers, we ponder.

A tapestry of twilight's weave,
In shadows deep, we believe.
The night's embrace, both warm and stark,
Guides the lost through the dark.

Passing Glances of Fallen Stars

When stars fall from heaven's embrace,
They leave behind a fleeting trace.
In the night, they twinkle so bright,
A dance of dreams in joyous flight.

Passing glances, a wish on high,
As we whisper secrets to the sky.
With each twinkle, a chance to change,
The cosmos shifts, both vast and strange.

Luminous paths through shadows weave,
An invitation for hearts to believe.
In the moments caught between breath,
A glimpse of magic, outrunning death.

Fallen stars, like tears of light,
Bring whispers of hope in the night.
For dreams reborn, we shout and cry,
As the universe winks goodbye.

Through celestial tides, we chase the gleam,
In every pulse, the thread of a dream.
With passing glances, our spirits soar,
Embracing wonders forevermore.

The Mirage of Shattered Laughter

Amidst the echoes, laughter fades,
In the silence, memory wades.
Happiness lost in the clamor,
A mirage wrapped in a glamour.

Once it danced, a glistening sound,
Now in whispers, it's unbound.
Fragments scattered like autumn leaves,
A tapestry of what one believes.

When laughter shatters, it sings a song,
Of fleeting moments where we belong.
In the heart, a flicker remains,
A glimmer of joy in the pains.

Through twilight's veil, we chase the past,
Clutching shadows that fade so fast.
In the mirage of shadow and light,
We find the echoes of pure delight.

So linger we must in these dreams,
Where laughter dances, or so it seems.
Rekindling joy in places dire,
Our hearts, ignited, leap ever higher.

Tracing the Tides of Embered Shadows

In the flickering light, shadows wait,
Tracing the tides of an unseen fate.
Embers glow with a whispered flame,
In the stillness, we call their name.

Each silhouette tells a story deep,
Of lost moments that time will keep.
Fading echoes of laughter and tears,
In the canvas of lingering years.

Through the night, our dreams take flight,
Wrapped in the cloak of the velvet night.
Chasing shadows, we forge our way,
Guided by stars that refuse to sway.

Embers flicker, their dance unconfined,
Mirroring tales of the heart entwined.
With each step, our spirits flow,
Tracing the paths where the wild winds blow.

As dawn unfurls her golden hues,
We gather stories from dusk's soft muse.
In embered shadows, life's truths align,
With tender grace, the stars will shine.

Laughs Cradled by Shimmering Night

In the hush of a moonlit glow,
Whispers dance where shadows go.
Soft laughter wraps the silent woods,
A symphony of playful moods.

Stars twinkle in the azure deep,
Cradled dreams begin to leap.
Echoes of joy in the air,
Nature holds her breath in prayer.

Glimmers paint the world in glee,
As fireflies flicker wild and free.
The night embraces with gentle arms,
A magic spun from hidden charms.

All worries fade in twilight's blend,
A reminder that joys can mend.
With laughter's light, we chase the fright,
As the night shimmers, pure and bright.

Together we weave a tapestry,
Of mirth and warmth, a wondrous sea.
In this realm where secrets hide,
We find our peace, as hearts collide.

Revelry Under the Tattered Sky

Beneath the rags of evening's cloak,
A chorus brews, a merry croak.
With laughter spilling from each nook,
We dance, as time itself we took.

Stars peek through the thin, torn veil,
As stories of old wind and trail.
The moon, our guide, so solemn yet bright,
Illuminates our fleeting flight.

Fires flicker, casting tales anew,
As shadows join in the dance we do.
With every beat, our spirits soar,
A celebration by night's door.

Mirthful echoes fill the air,
As magic lingers everywhere.
We sing to the realms of dreams untold,
Transforming night into pure gold.

In the chaos of jubilant cries,
We find our truth beneath rough skies.
For in this joy, no heart shall lie,
We revel bold, under night's eye.

Mirth on the Edge of Dusk

As the sun dips below the line,
Whispers tease the edges fine.
Laughter spills like summer rain,
Chasing shadows in the plain.

The horizon blushes, a tender hue,
Gathering dreams like morning dew.
In twilight's grip, we find our place,
A gentle pause, a warm embrace.

Swaying to the rhythm of night,
With every echo, hearts take flight.
In this fleeting, magic hour,
We bloom like a midnight flower.

Chasing colors that softly blend,
Mirth surrounds, no need to pretend.
For on this brink, the world feels small,
And laughter rises, covering all.

Let's gather memories, weave them tight,
In the tapestry of falling light.
With every chuckle, and every sigh,
We paint the dusk, as night draws nigh.

The Lethargic Spin of Time's Wheel

In the quiet hum of an old clock's song,
Time lingers, where dreams belong.
Each tick a whisper, soft and slow,
Carrying secrets where few dare go.

Days drift like leaves on a gentle stream,
Caught in a weave of a timeless dream.
With every glance, the world feels heavy,
Yet fleeting moments shimmer steady.

We tread the paths of silent grace,
As hours melt in a warm embrace.
A hesitant dance on the edge of fate,
Where every heartbeat seems to wait.

In the space between dusk and dawn,
We ponder what has come and gone.
With weary eyes, we dare to see,
The beauty held in lethargy.

So let us sway with the spinning wheel,
And cherish the curve of time's appeal.
For in this stillness, we find our way,
Embracing life's soft ballet.

The Enigma of Softly Fading Flames

In the twilight's gentle sigh,
Flickers dance and softly die,
Secrets whispered on the breeze,
Lost among the autumn leaves.

Each ember glows with muted grace,
A fleeting spark, a tender trace,
Memories wrapped in shadow's cloak,
Of whispered words that go unspoken.

The shadows stretch, they twist and twirl,
In the dimming light, they swirl,
A riddle held in amber hues,
The night's embrace, a silent muse.

Though darkness veils what once was bright,
Hope lingers on in the fading light,
As embers warm the night's retreat,
A promise found, a soul's heartbeat.

So listen close, let stillness guide,
The secrets in the flames reside,
For in each flicker's soft demise,
A world of wonder softly lies.

Whirling Dreams in the Embered Night

In the hush of velvet skies,
Dreams take flight on whispered sighs,
Amidst the glow of fading stars,
In mystic realms, where magic spars.

A nightingale sings soft and low,
To serenade the flames' warm glow,
Each flicker tells a tale untold,
Of chasms deep and hearts so bold.

As shadows dance in quiet pools,
The world transforms to dreamlike rules,
With every whisper, every flick,
They swirl and weave, a cosmic trick.

In embered light, the visions sway,
Painting tales in a wondrous way,
Where every spark ignites the dawn,
And leaves behind the night's soft yawn.

So chase the dreams in twilight's grasp,
Hold on tight; let magic clasp,
For in the embered night so dear,
Lies the pulse of dreams we bear.

When Shadows Play with Ember's Glow

When shadows stretch and softly sway,
They whisper secrets of the day,
In ember's glow, they dance with glee,
A ballet of what used to be.

With every flicker, every spark,
They conjure warmth within the dark,
A flickering light that dares to dream,
In twilight's hush, a silent gleam.

The world is hushed, a still embrace,
As shadows waltz with tender grace,
In the heart of night, they softly play,
The music of the fading day.

As embers sigh and softly fade,
The dance of shadows gently laid,
Echoes of warmth, a sweet refrain,
In every glow, love's soft gain.

So linger here, in this warm thrall,
With shadows playing, let hearts befall,
For in the glow of fleeting light,
Lies the magic of the night.

The Lost Serenade of the Searing Dawn

In dawn's embrace, where shadows flee,
A serenade sings to the sea,
In every ray that breaks the night,
A tale unfolds in golden light.

With each step of the waking sun,
Lost melodies begin to run,
Whispers dance on the morning breeze,
A harmony that seeks to please.

But some notes linger just behind,
Trapped in echoes of the mind,
A haunting song that calls the lost,
In the glow of dawn, there's a cost.

As light unfolds, the past takes flight,
And whispers weave with day and night,
The serenade, though bittersweet,
Pulls at hearts that yearn to meet.

Yet as the sun ascends above,
Each note, it carries loss and love,
For in the dawn, the shadows stay,
A serenade of yesterday.

Secrets of the Gloomy Enclave

In the shadows where whispers reside,
Secrets dwell, and dreams often hide.
Ancient trees with branches bent low,
Guard the tales of long ago.

In the corners of the winding paths,
Echoes linger of forgotten laughs.
Moonlight dances on dewy leaves,
Telling stories that time weaves.

In the breeze, there's a calling tune,
Sung by the soft glow of the moon.
Lurking mysteries, hidden so tight,
Await the brave souls who seek the light.

A flicker here, a shimmer there,
The heart quickens; the world feels rare.
Voices murmur, a gentle plea,
Unlock the secrets, set them free.

Beneath the cloak of night's embrace,
The Enclave guards its sacred space.
With every step, the magic swells,
For in the dark, the spirit dwells.

Beneath the Guardian's Gaze

High above, the stars glimmer bright,
A guardian watches over the night.
With wisdom born from ages past,
Keeping watch till the dawn at last.

In shadows where the lost souls tread,
He whispers softly, guiding the dread.
With every heartbeat, a spark ignites,
Revealing paths hidden from sights.

The mountains echo the secrets told,
By ancient spirits, both wise and bold.
They weave a web of twilight's charm,
To shield the seekers from all harm.

Under the gaze, the brave dare roam,
Each step they take brings them closer to home.
In the silence, a promise rings true,
Beneath the guardian, they start anew.

As dawn breaks soft with hues of gold,
The tales unfold, the stories told.
In the light of day, they find their way,
Guided by courage, come what may.

Muffled Laughter in the Cinder Grove

In the heart of the whispering trees,
Laughter dances on a gentle breeze.
Amidst the ashes where dreams may dwell,
Muffled giggles cast a curious spell.

Flickering flames in the quiet night,
Share the glow of stories alight.
In the warmth of the cinder's embrace,
Memories linger, a tender trace.

Ghosts of merriment, sweet and bold,
Rekindle laughter from tales retold.
Though shadows linger and night feels long,
In the grove, the heart beats strong.

Each rustling leaf, a chuckle shared,
Echoes of joy, remnants declared.
In the stillness, where spirits roam,
The cinder grove feels like home.

So gather 'round, let your laughter rise,
Fill the night with your sweet reprise.
For in this grove, under starlit skies,
Muffled joy is never disguised.

Chasing Smoke in the Lurking Night

In the chill of the lurking night,
Smoke curls softly, a ghostly flight.
Whispers trace through the air so thin,
A pursuit begins, where dreams have been.

Chasing shadows that dart and weave,
Each turn a secret we all believe.
With every breath, the mystery grows,
As the night reveals what nobody knows.

Footsteps echo on cobbled stone,
In the silence, a heart feels alone.
Yet with the fog, a promise beckons,
Of tales entwined, of unseen reckonings.

In the depths, a flicker, a glow,
Leads the way where the lost souls go.
Chasing smoke into the dark, profound,
In their pursuit, new magic is found.

With dawn's first light, the chase will wane,
Yet the echoes of night will still remain.
In the heart of shadows, the truth shall glide,
Beneath the stars, where dreams abide.

The Enchanted Lanterns of the Burnt Yet Bold

In the stillness of the night, they gleam,
Lanterns flicker, weaving dreams.
Burnt edges tell a tale of old,
Of courage bright and spirits bold.

Amidst the shadows, their light does dance,
Guiding the lost with a hopeful glance.
Each spark ignites a memory deep,
Whispering secrets for souls to keep.

They rise from ashes, glowing gold,
With stories of valor yet untold.
Through tangled woods and whispering streams,
They beckon forth both hopes and dreams.

This night, we gather, hearts entwined,
By enchanted beacons, where souls are defined.
With every flicker, we share our plight,
In the soft embrace of the tranquil night.

So lift your eyes, to the stars above,
Bound by the lanterns, wrapped in love.
For in their glow, the burnt yet bold,
Find solace rich, a warmth to hold.

Tales of Merriment by Charred Glimmers

In the dawn of dusk, laughter arises,
From charred glimmers, wild and wise.
Echoes of revelry pierce the haze,
Reviving joy in the smoky maze.

With ragged banners and embers bright,
We gather 'round in soft twilight.
Tales of merriment, spun with cheer,
Ring through the hearts that gather near.

For every laughter lost to the flame,
Resurrects anew, never quite the same.
In each crackle, a spirit flies,
Chasing shadows, donning disguise.

O'er charred remains, we weave our fate,
With smiles igniting, erasing hate.
In every glance, a moment found,
As whispers of magic wrap around.

So dance tonight beside the glow,
Of charred glimmers, letting hearts flow.
In the bonds of laughter, we shall find,
The tales of merriment intertwined.

Graffiti of Joy on Smoldered Walls

Upon the walls where shadows weep,
Graffiti blooms, bright and deep.
Colorful strokes on surfaces bare,
Whispers of joy linger in the air.

With every splash, a story unfolds,
Of dreams rebuilt, and hearts made bold.
Through flashes of paint, the past we claim,
Finding beauty within the flame.

These smoldered walls, a gallery vast,
Holding the future, healing the past.
Each vivid hue a promise to keep,
Awakening hope from slumbered sleep.

With laughter sketched in colorful lines,
We dance on remnants where sunlight shines.
For every tear that has rolled and fell,
An artwork lives, a tale to tell.

Embrace the joy in strokes that gleam,
For graffiti is life, it's the heart's dream.
Beyond the smolder, we stand so tall,
As the story of joy adorns the wall.

The Vignette of Lost Laughs Among Ash

Amongst the ash, where shadows dwell,
Lie lost laughs in a silent shell.
A vignette captured, a fleeting grace,
In memory's eyes, they find their place.

With echoes of mirth, the air is thick,
Reminders of joy that now feel quick.
Each whisper of laughter, a breeze from the past,
In the heart's gallery, their echo will last.

Through stillness and silence, we wander slow,
Tracing the lines where the laughter would flow.
In gentle reverie, we claim each sound,
For lost laughter still lingers, richly profound.

So sift through the ash, let memories rise,
In the echoes of joy, find the spark in your eyes.
For though they were lost, they shimmer and sway,
In heartbeats of hope, they forever will play.

With nods to the past, we gather anew,
With stories of laughter, the bold and the true.
Amongst the ash, let their warmth be found,
In the vignette of lost laughs, forever unbound.

Recollection of Joy Under Winged Terrors

In skies adorned with shadows wide,
The echoes of laughter, once our guide,
Fleeting moments, pure and bright,
Now tremble beneath the fading light.

Yet memories, like stars that gleam,
In quiet corners of a dream,
Whisper tales of joy and cheer,
Even when dark wings draw near.

With every beat of a heart so wild,
The laughter of the lost, like a child,
Reminds me of the times we soared,
While winged terrors, fate's accord.

So let the winds of memory sway,
In hues of dawn, the fears decay,
For joy, like magic, never dies,
And in our hearts, forever lies.

Hold tight those strands of golden past,
As shadows filter, ebb and cast,
For even under winged despair,
Joy's soft whispers linger in the air.

Crossroads of Silenced Revelry

At the crossroad where shadows meet,
Where laughter fades, and echoes retreat,
We stand in silence, hearts entwined,
In the hush, lost joys we find.

The night once danced with vibrant cheer,
Now stillness cloaks the atmosphere,
Yet memories hum a gentle tune,
Beneath the pale gaze of the moon.

Footfalls linger on cobblestone,
Whispers of revelry, now overthrown,
In this realm where silence reigns,
The spirit of joy still remains.

With every heartbeat, shadows wane,
Inviting echoes of joy's refrain,
Fractured laughter from days of yore,
Fills the air like a phantom score.

So let us linger at this forked way,
In reverence to light that won't decay,
For in the stillness, our hearts align,
At the crossroads of time, love will shine.

Vestiges of Flame in an Endless Dance

In the twilight where embers sigh,
Flickering softly as day bids goodbye,
Vestiges of flame, a dance so grand,
Whisper stories from a trembling hand.

Around the fire, shadows weave,
In the glow of hope, we believe,
Emotions swirl like sparks in flight,
An endless dance in the arms of night.

With every flicker, memories blaze,
Remnants of warmth in a smoky haze,
Past and present interlace their grace,
In the heart's chamber, they find their place.

Though time may dim, the fire persists,
In the twilight's keep, it still exists,
In every gust, in every sway,
The flame ignites, the shadows play.

So let us cherish this dance divine,
With vestiges of flame forever shine,
For in the stories of each heart's trance,
Lies an echo of love's endless dance.

Fables of Shadow Beneath Draughts of Smoke

In the haze where whispers blend,
Fables of shadow, around the bend,
Stories curled in the tendrils gray,
Drift like echoes from yesterday.

Beneath the smoke, the truth lies bare,
Shadows waltz in the frigid air,
With every sigh, a lesson learned,
In the quiet gloom, the lanterns burned.

These tales of wonder, of heart and strife,
Meld with the fabric of our life,
Though shrouded in dim and dusky yoke,
Each word is a flicker, a spark, a stroke.

Let us weave these stories tight,
In the arms of darkness, there is light,
For fables told in smoky rooms,
Hold the essence of blooming blooms.

So gather 'round, in shadows cast,
Embrace the fables, hold them fast,
For in the draughts of smoke and lore,
Lives the pulse of the tales we adore.

Beneath the Scales of Faded Glory

In shadows deep where echoes blend,
A serpent's tale begins to bend.
Its scales, once bright, now dulled by time,
Whisper secrets, lost in rhyme.

A castle looms on crumbling stone,
Where visions fade, yet dreams have grown.
The past entwined with ancient lore,
Awaits the heart that dares explore.

Through twisted paths of magic's thread,
The whispers call of those long dead.
In twilight's grasp, the truth will shine,
Beneath the scales, a fate divine.

Once grand halls where laughter roamed,
Now silence wraps the hearts it combed.
Yet hope flickers in darkened halls,
As courage rises, softly calls.

So tread with care, dear soul so brave,
In the heart of what the shadows crave.
For in the depths of faded nights,
Lies glory hidden, holding lights.

The Quiet Thrill of Hidden Brawls

In moonlit corners secrets stir,
Where whispers clash and tempests purr.
A flick of wrist, the air ignites,
With quiet thrills, the dusk ignites.

Beneath the gaze of masked intent,
Each heartbeat drums with firm dissent.
Fingers lace behind the veil,
Of battles fought where spirits sail.

The dance of shadows, risk entwined,
In silence, truths and lies combined.
A shuffle here, a glance askew,
In hidden brawls, what will unfold anew?

Explosive joy in every clash,
As laughter bursts, then fades in a flash.
No rules, no bounds, just daring flights,
In secret nights, where time ignites.

So raise your glass, let spirits soar,
For life is but a whispered roar.
Embrace the thrill, let senses twine,
In hidden brawls, the stars align.

Dreams Entangled in Dusky Veils

In dusky veils where shadows creep,
The dreams of night begin to leap.
Whispers weave through silken strands,
Of hopes entwined in gentle hands.

With every sigh, a tale is spun,
Of worlds unfurling, battles won.
Through claret skies and twilight's glow,
The pulse of magic starts to flow.

A lantern's light on paths unknown,
Reveals the heart's most secret tone.
So tread with grace where shadows dance,
In every dream lies a chance.

The pulse of starlight beckons near,
A symphony for those who hear.
In dusky veils, embrace the night,
For dreams await with pure delight.

So close your eyes, let visions spin,
In tangled fates, your soul within.
For in the dark, there's life anew,
Dreams entangled, waiting for you.

Fables of the Mirthless Masquerade

In halls adorned with masks and grace,
Where smiles hide a shadowed face.
A fable spins of joy and woe,
In mirthless dance, the secrets grow.

With every glance, a story weaves,
Tales of heartache, hope deceives.
Laughter rings with hollow sound,
In masquerade, truth's seldom found.

Beneath the glimmer, doubts abide,
As hearts mask fears they cannot bide.
In twisted jest, the night unfolds,
With hidden truths that fate foretold.

When dawn arrives, the masks will fall,
Revealing bonds that bind us all.
But here within the twilight's paint,
Fables rise with mysteries quaint.

So join the dance of veils and guise,
Amidst the laughter, hear the cries.
In mirthless masquerade, we play,
Where life's own fables find their way.

Silhouettes Against the Glowing Sky

In twilight's grasp, the shadows dance,
A fleeting glimpse, a timeless chance.
Figures wreathed in hues of fire,
Whispers soft, as dreams conspire.

Beneath the stars, they weave and sway,
Echoes of night in soft array.
The world holds breath, in awe they stand,
In silhouette, a secret band.

The horizon blushes, cloaked in gold,
Stories of old in silence told.
With every shape that bends and twines,
A tale is spun, where fate aligns.

And as the sun bids light goodbye,
The silhouettes against the sky,
Invite the dreamers to their side,
Where magic blooms and hearts confide.

In the hush of night, their spirits rise,
Illuminated by starlit skies.
A dance of shadows, free and wild,
In every heart, a hopeful child.

Wandering Souls in the Distant Flames

Through night's embrace, they roam and weave,
Seeking the warmth that shadows leave.
With flickering lights as their guiding stars,
The wandering souls carry their scars.

In glowing embers where lost dreams lie,
They whisper secrets, no need to cry.
Each flame a beacon, each spark a sigh,
Together they wander, together they fly.

Through realms forgotten, on whispered breeze,
In ancient woods where time does freeze.
They spin in circles, eternally bound,
In the dance of the night, they are profound.

As shadows twist 'neath the watchful moon,
They find their rhythm, a haunting tune.
Resilience breathes in the flickering light,
In distant flames, they conquer the night.

With souls entwined, they chase the dawn,
A tapestry woven, where hope is drawn.
And in each flicker, there lies a tale,
Of wandering souls who fear no gale.

The Silent Imprint of Scales

In twilight's grip, a tale unfolds,
Of ancient beasts and secrets told.
Upon the earth, their shadows lay,
The silent imprint, a ghostly fray.

With scales like armor, glistening bright,
They roamed the realms, a wondrous sight.
Each step a whisper, soft yet grand,
A legacy etched upon the land.

The echoes linger, in forgotten dreams,
Lost in the flow of time's swift streams.
Through ages past, their spirits soar,
In every heartbeat, they are evermore.

Beneath the stars, their stories glide,
In swirls of mist, no need to hide.
They leave their mark, both fierce and true,
In every heart, a memory new.

The world remembers those timeless trails,
Unseen, unheard, the silent scales.
In whispered lore and moonlit skies,
The imprint endures, never dies.

Lament of the Enchanted Abyss

Deep in the depths where silence reigns,
A mournful sigh, like phantom chains.
The enchanted abyss, a world apart,
Holds shadows of love, despair in art.

Echoes of voices, lost in the deep,
In swirling currents, dreams drift and weep.
From coral thrones to star-cloaked seams,
The lament rises on midnight streams.

Beneath the waves where time suspends,
A haunting song, as fate descends.
With every ripple, a story swells,
In the heart of darkness, magic dwells.

And in the silence, a truth is found,
In every tear, the past is crowned.
The abyss cradles each whispered fate,
In tender arms, they resonate.

As dreams converge in watery sighs,
The enchantment lingers, never dies.
A tale unfolding, lost in the mist,
In the abyss's heart, love's eternal twist.

The Unseen Flicker of a Fading Flame

In shadows deep where silence weeps,
A flicker stirs, a secret keeps.
Amidst the night, it wanes in flight,
A pulse of warmth, a fading light.

Whispers crawl where dreams reside,
In corners dim, the heart's denied.
Each breath of dusk, a tender pull,
An ember glows, though time is dull.

Forgotten tales that linger near,
The stories spun from threads of fear.
Yet hope remains, though time does fade,
In every spark, a promise made.

So hold the flame, let it ignite,
For every night must bow to light.
A wound may ache, but love can mend,
In shadows cast, we find a friend.

With every flicker, wisdom grows,
In twilight's breath, the stillness flows.
Embrace the glow, though small it seems,
In the unseen, we find our dreams.

Whimsy Lurking in Stagnant Waters

In crystal pools where ripples lie,
A dance of dreams, where fancies fly.
Beneath the calm, the mischief stirs,
Life's laughter trapped, yet softly purrs.

The lilies float like thoughts untold,
Each petal whispers secrets bold.
In stillness deep, the stories twist,
A playful wisp, a fleeting tryst.

Among the reeds, the fairies weave,
A tapestry of joys to cleave.
With every glance, the magic sways,
In stagnant depths, the heart obeys.

Yet time moves on, the current swirls,
And whimsy's touch brings fleeting pearls.
In muddy beds, the wonders rest,
The quiet laughter, a playful jest.

So take a leap, embrace the mirth,
In tranquil tides, we find our worth.
For deep within stagnation's grasp,
Lies whimsy's touch, a joyful clasp.

Where Jests Turn to Whispers

Beneath the stars where laughter played,
A jest was born, a joke delayed.
Yet moments shift, the jest turns frail,
As shadows move, the echoes pale.

In corners dark, the whispers creep,
Where laughter lived, the silence weeps.
A punchline lost, a tale retold,
The heart's mirth fades, the truth unfolds.

The playful banter now subdued,
Each word a brush, each tone imbued.
In secrets shared, a bond once dear,
Now twisted fate ignites the fear.

Yet in the quiet, glimmers still,
A memory bright, an ancient thrill.
For every jest that turns to cry,
Holds laughter's ghost, a soft goodbye.

So let us tread where echoes play,
In shadows cast by light of day.
For jests may wane, but softly hum,
In whispers shared, the joy will come.

Mirrors of Enchantment and Sorrow

In silver glass, reflections gleam,
A world of wonder, a fleeting dream.
Each visage worn, a tale to spin,
Both joy and pain rest deep within.

The shimmer hides the heart's true lore,
In secret depths, whispered evermore.
With every glance, a truth revealed,
The magic's touch, a wound unsealed.

But sorrow dwells in graceful lines,
Each tear a story, a soul's designs.
In mirrored depths, the heart does mend,
Through trials faced, we find a friend.

Yet in the cracks, enchantment calls,
A chance to rise when darkness falls.
For every loss, a chance to see,
The strength within, to set us free.

So peer within, embrace the grace,
For mirrors hold our truest place.
In joy and sorrow, the echo stirs,
In every heart, enchantment purrs.

Hushed Retreat from the Ember's Thrall

In shadows deep where embers fade,
The whispering winds of twilight wade.
A heart once bold begins to quail,
As night descends upon the trail.

Through tangled woods where silence sighs,
The moonlight dances, softly lies.
Lost in thought, the pathways blur,
A secret kept, a silent stir.

The flickering light retreats from sight,
As starlit dreams take gentle flight.
Yet somewhere, hope begins to swell,
In the echo of a distant bell.

With every step, the embers gleam,
A flicker catches, reignites the dream.
From ash and darkness, strength reborn,
In the hush of dusk, new path is worn.

So let the shadows swirl and dance,
For in their grip, there lies romance.
A choice to make, we tread with care,
A hush retreats from ember's glare.

Flickering Hopes in the Dragon's Lair

Beneath the peak where dragons soar,
Lies a lair of myths and lore.
With scales that shimmer, eyes aglow,
A place where only brave hearts go.

In quiet corners, hopes ignite,
Flickering softly in the night.
The tales of old, both fierce and grand,
Whisper dreams of a distant land.

Through crackling fire, souls confer,
Secrets shared in a gentle stir.
For every heart that dares to dream,
In the dragon's eye, there's a gleam.

Yet shadows loom, a weighty breath,
In this lair of life and death.
But courage blooms like flowers bold,
As flickering hopes bring tales retold.

So gather round, let stories weave,
In the warmth of the lair, we believe.
For dragons sleep, but dreams take flight,
In the flickering hopes of the night.

Beneath the Canopy of Scales and Dreams

Beneath the coils of ages past,
Where echoes swirl and shadows cast.
A canopy of dreams entwined,
In scales of silver, secrets bind.

The whispers rustle through the air,
A world beyond, both bright and rare.
With every breath, a tale unfolds,
Of bravery and hearts of gold.

In twilight's glow, the path is clear,
Guided by hope, we banish fear.
The stars above begin to sing,
Of distant realms and wondrous things.

Among the scales, a warmth resides,
In dreams we forge, where love abides.
To chase the dawn with spirits high,
As lanterns pulse beneath the sky.

So take my hand, let's venture through,
Beneath the canopy, ever true.
For in this realm of dreams and light,
We find our courage, shining bright.

Echoes of the Hearth Beneath Starlit Scales

In the hearth where embers glow,
Whispers stir, the softest flow.
Beneath the stars, with scales unfurled,
Echoes of magic, a hidden world.

Each flicker sings of stories old,
Of brave hearts warm and spirits bold.
A gathering round, we share our fates,
As dreams intertwine, the night awaits.

Through tales of yore, the flames will leap,
In every murmur, memories seep.
With laughter bright, the shadows play,
As starlit scales guide our way.

The soothing glow a balm to hearts,
In this haven where the journey starts.
We weave our lives in threads of light,
As echoes dance into the night.

So let us gather, side by side,
In whispers sweet, our dreams reside.
For in the hearth, with starlit scales,
Our stories linger, where magic prevails.

Echoes of Forgotten Escapades

In the corners of dreams, whispers call,
Footsteps echo down the shadowed hall.
Fragments of laughter linger like light,
Memories twirl in the cool, soft night.

Worn-out maps tell tales of yore,
Journeys taken through unseen doors.
A flicker of magic, a flash of glee,
In every heartbeat, a bold decree.

Forgotten paths of wonder and spin,
Lost in the stories, we find the kin.
Adventures hidden in starlit views,
Beneath the tapestry of midnight hues.

With a wave of the wand, the echoes revive,
In the treasure of old, our spirits thrive.
Together we danced on the edge of the world,
While dreams of escape around us swirled.

So gather the echoes, let's weave them clear,
For the magic of life is forever near.
In the shifting shadows, where stories dwell,
We charm the night with our whispered spell.

When Joy Meets the Weight of Shadows

In the dance of the dusk, where dreams collide,
Joy flutters softly, though shadows abide.
Laughter breaks through like a songbird's call,
Yet lurking behind it, a curtain so tall.

Each smile a treasure, so precious and bright,
Yet tinged with the hues of the encroaching night.
Hope glimmers gently, a flickered flame,
Yet shadows stretch long, whispering names.

In the heart of the storm, where laughter is spun,
Weight of the shadows can dim the sun.
Yet still, we find strength in the burden we share,
For light mingles warmly with shadowed despair.

Through the veil of the evening, a promise we weave,
That joy is a dance, and in struggle, we believe.
For every tear sheds a glimmering light,
A reminder that hope must still bloom in night.

So let us embrace both the joy and the gloom,
For life's sweetest moments arise from the tomb.
In the hush of the twilight, we find a way,
To carry our shadows and dance through the gray.

The Clumsy Waltz of Lost Adventures

In the muddled midst of a misstep or two,
Clumsy hearts twirl beneath skies deep and blue.
With laughter erupting like bubbles of air,
We stumble through meadows, unburdened by care.

Each path that we take, a whimsical fate,
Turning between twirls, we challenge the weight.
Falling like leaves in the crisp autumn's breath,
Where joy meets the folly, we court our own death.

For every wrong turn leads to treasures untold,
With stories of daring stitched in the bold.
Adventures forgotten beckon from afar,
In the clumsy waltz beneath twilight's star.

With hearts full of wonder, let's trip hand in hand,
In a dance that is anchored on whimsies so grand.
Every fall a reminder that laughter can soar,
As we twirl through the memories and seek to explore.

So here's to the stumbles that light up our way,
In the grand orchestration of life's vast ballet.
We waltz with the clumsy, with hearts full of glee,
As we weave through the stories of what's meant to be.

Stories Woven in Twilight's Fabric

In twilight's embrace, where shadows entwine,
Stories are whispered, like aged, solemn wine.
Each thread a connection, a moment preserved,
In the fabric of time, our destinies curved.

With fingers like starlight, we stitch and we sew,
From fragments of laughter, the colors do glow.
A tapestry woven with hearts as the loom,
In the weft of the night, dreams blossom and bloom.

Each tale a reminder, a flicker of grace,
In the depths of our journeys, we find our own place.
Little lanterns of wisdom guide paths unseen,
As we dance through the echoes of what might have been.

Together we wander through shades of the dusk,
In the warmth of the stories, our hearts feel the husk.
For woven in twilight, we find our own light,
As the whispers of ages wrap softly around night.

So gather the threads, let us craft with delight,
For the stories we share make the darkness feel bright.
In each woven moment, a universe grows,
As we bask in the magic that twilight bestows.

In the Wake of Smoldered Ruins

In the wake of smoldered ruins,
Ghosts whisper through the haze.
Flickering shadows dance alone,
In the echoes of lost days.

What once stood noble, proud, and tall,
Now crumbles into dust.
The heartbeats of a past so grand,
Are buried in the rust.

Amidst the fading ember glow,
A story waits to rise.
From ashes, hope may yet return,
Beneath the starlit skies.

Each stone has tales of laughter's song,
And secrets we explore.
Beneath the quiet, slumbering night,
There lies forevermore.

Let not despair consume the dreams,
For from the ruins true,
New life shall sprout, as time will weave,
A tapestry anew.

Cinders Whispering Forgotten Tales

Cinders whispering forgotten tales,
Of knights and ladies fair.
In the twilight's soft embrace,
Magic lingers in the air.

Echoed laughter, echoes long,
Haunt these ancient walls.
In every crack, a lingering song,
In every breeze, it calls.

Flames once danced with fervent pride,
Now simmer in the night.
Yet hope remains amongst the ash,
To spark the dark to light.

Tread softly where the shadows steal,
For dangers linger still.
But where there's fire, there's a soul,
Resilient, warm, and chill.

Through the cinders, dreams revive,
In whispers soft and clear.
The past unfolds, a tale to tell,
For those who dare to hear.

The Quietus of Charred Glades

The quietus of charred glades,
Whilst silence holds its breath.
A solemn peace rests lightly here,
In the embrace of death.

Amongst the blackened branches bare,
Life waits with bated hope.
Tender shoots creep through the ash,
An emerald, fragile rope.

Each glance reveals a haunting past,
Yet beauty finds a way.
From lifeless earth, new dreams will sprout,
And turn to bright array.

The starlight spills on what remains,
In silver pools of night.
A promise made by nature's hand,
To heal what once took flight.

With every dawn, the forest stirs,
Each whisper tells of time.
In charred glades, both loss and gain,
Compose a sacred rhyme.

Beneath Wings of the Enduring Night

Beneath wings of the enduring night,
Where dreams are shrouded deep,
The stars alight with whispered hope,
While weary shadows creep.

In the hush of dark, a solace found,
A place where silence reigns.
The world transforms in twilight's arms,
Its magic refrains.

With eyes that glimmer, darkness cradles,
All secrets held so tight.
Behind the veil, a luminescence,
Awaits the break of light.

For every fear that haunts the heart,
There thrums a spirit bold.
In the depths of night, we gather strength,
For stories yet untold.

So let the night enfold your dreams,
In shadows soft and wide.
Beneath its wings, we will take flight,
Together, side by side.